CONTENTS

ON THE MOVE

Have you ever had to move anything
large, heavy and awkward?
How did you manage?

How do you think these
things could be moved?

You use forces in several ways when you are playing. Where are the forces?

Think of some of the other games you play. Draw some of your own pictures showing where the forces are.

3

LIFE FORCE

There are many things in nature that are far stronger than those made by people.

Next time you are out in the woods, pick up two dead branches and see how long you can hold them up over your head. Imagine how strong a tree must be to hold up all those branches.

Some bamboo stems are strong enough to use as **scaffolding**.

The thread in a spider's web is far stronger than fine steel wire of the same thickness. What happens if just one strand of a web is broken?

Animals can also be very strong.

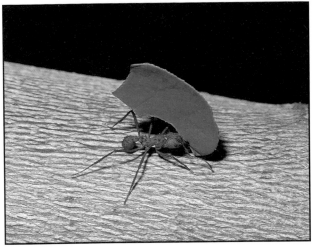

An ant can move fifty times its own body weight.

A thrush bangs a snail on a rock to break its shell.

Male stags fight by charging at each other, clashing their antlers. Fossils of dinosaurs have been found with very strong skulls. Imagine the forces involved when they charged at each other!

Wow! Did you know that a woman standing in shoes with stiletto heels presses harder on the ground than an elephant in bare feet!

A CHANGE OF DIRECTION

When dentists began filling teeth over a hundred years ago, they needed a small but fast drill to take out the bad parts of the teeth. Imagine trying to drill a back tooth with one of these!

All sorts of strange inventions were tried, including a clockwork drill.

Then in 1872 a dentist called James Morrison invented a drill driven by a pedal which turned a big **pulley**. The cord round the pulley passed along an arm to another pulley which turned the drill. The arm had **hinges** with smaller pulleys at the joints, so that the drill could be moved to any position or angle.

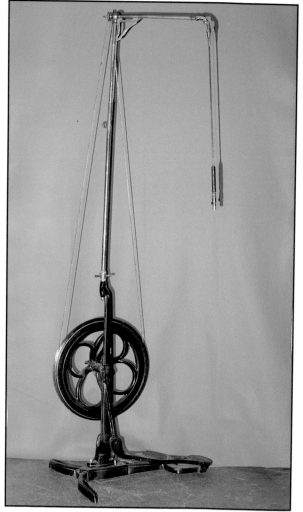

Making forces go round corners has always been difficult. **Cogs** and **gears** are often used to change the direction or speed of a force.

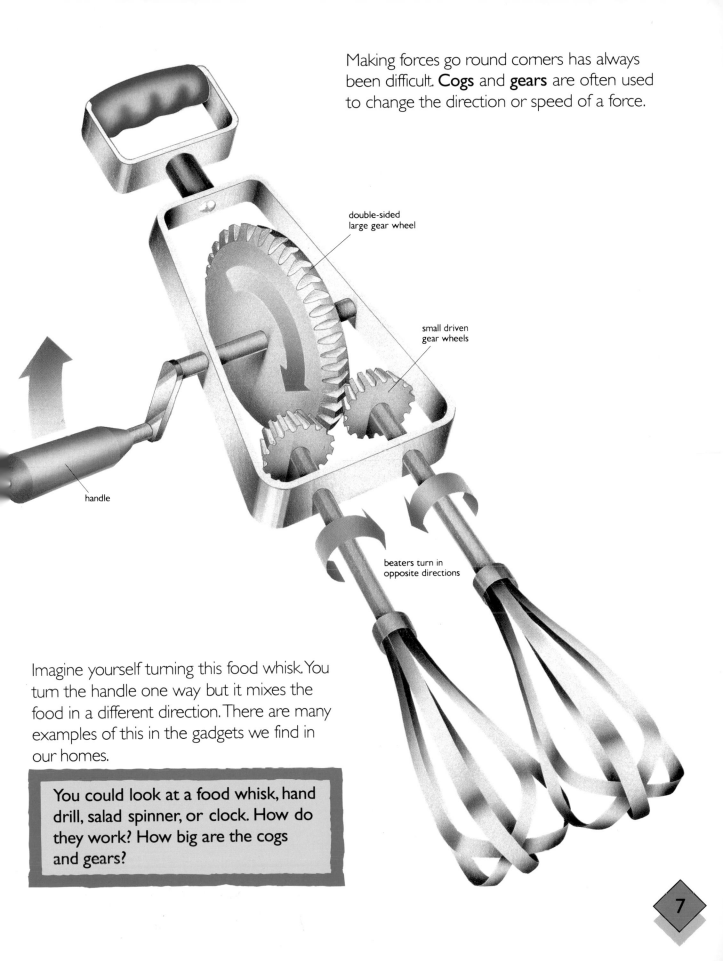

double-sided large gear wheel

small driven gear wheels

handle

beaters turn in opposite directions

Imagine yourself turning this food whisk. You turn the handle one way but it mixes the food in a different direction. There are many examples of this in the gadgets we find in our homes.

You could look at a food whisk, hand drill, salad spinner, or clock. How do they work? How big are the cogs and gears?

LIFTING AND SHIFTING THINGS

John made a den from a large wooden crate. His friend Anna suggested that it would be a good tree house. Their problem was how to get John's tree house up into the tree. Look at the pictures and tell the story. You might use some of these words; pull, push, turn, swing, hoist, **pulley**, press down, rub, snap.

What do you think they should be careful about?

JET PROPULSION

If you push something backwards you are pushed forwards. For instance, if you stand on rollerskates or a skateboard and throw something backwards, you will move forwards.

When a rocket is set off, the mixture inside it explodes and a rush of gas comes out at the tail. As the gas rushes backwards, the rocket shoots forwards.

Jet aircraft have huge blades which suck air in at the front and push it out behind with a powerful thrust. The aircraft moves forwards in the opposite direction to the thrust.

Jet aircraft are often blamed for damaging the environment. Can you think why? Consider things like fuel, noise and pollution. How could jets be improved? What about space rockets?

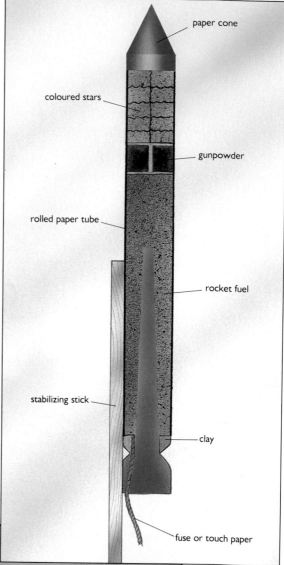

paper cone

coloured stars

gunpowder

rolled paper tube

rocket fuel

stabilizing stick

clay

fuse or touch paper

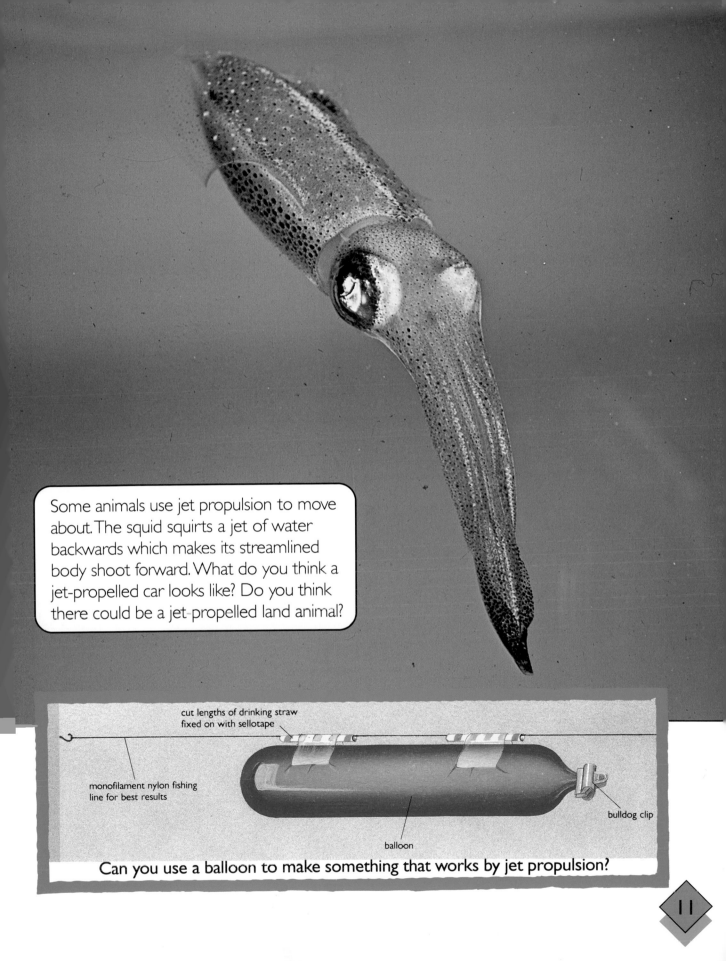

Some animals use jet propulsion to move about. The squid squirts a jet of water backwards which makes its streamlined body shoot forward. What do you think a jet-propelled car looks like? Do you think there could be a jet-propelled land animal?

cut lengths of drinking straw fixed on with sellotape

monofilament nylon fishing line for best results

bulldog clip

balloon

Can you use a balloon to make something that works by jet propulsion?

BUILDING BRIDGES

Even things that aren't moving are still being pushed and pulled.

A well-built bridge will stand for centuries because all the pushing and pulling forces in its structure balance out.

A suspension bridge

Where are the pushes and pulls on this bridge?

What do you think makes this bridge strong?

The great nineteenth-century engineer Isambard Kingdom Brunel was the son of March Brunel, another famous engineer. After being educated in France he joined his father in his work and was involved in the scheme for building a tunnel under the Thames. He went on to build many great structures including The Clifton Suspension Bridge and the Tamar Bridge which are still in use.

Fourteenth-century bridge in Kent.

Clifton Suspension Bridge near Bristol.

Tamar Bridge near Plymouth.

13

THE HOVERCRAFT

The first **hovercraft** was developed in the 1950s by the British inventor Christopher Cockerell. He started building and inventing things when he was a child. His father used to offer a £10 reward for every new thing he invented. (£10 was worth more in those days!) He developed the 'hover' idea when he was trying to find ways of making boats go faster.

Hovercraft are now used in many places and for different reasons. Why do you think they are used in the place shown here?

What do you think are the advantages and disadvantages of a hovercraft compared with other vehicles?

A huge fan draws air in through a funnel and pushes it out hard underneath.

The blast of air raises the craft up off the ground or water on a 'cushion' of air.

Why do you think the flexible rubber 'skirt' is important?

Can you see how the hovercraft is steered and what makes it move along?

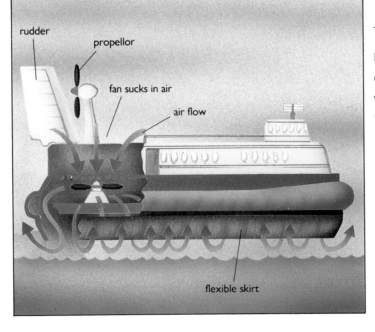

rudder

propellor

fan sucks in air

air flow

flexible skirt

TWISTING AND TURNING

Twistable Turnable Man

He's the Twistable Turnable
Squeezable Pullable Stretchable Foldable Man.
He can crawl in your pocket or fit in your locket
Or screw himself into a twenty-volt socket,
Or stretch himself up to the steeple or taller,
Or squeeze himself into a thimble or smaller,
Yes he can, course, he can,
He's the Twistable Turnable
Squeezable Pullable Stretchable
Shrinkable Man.
And he lives a passable life
With his Squeezable Lovable,
Kissable, Hugable, Pullable, Tugable Wife.
And they have two twistable kids
Who bend up the way that they did.
And they turn and they stretch
Just as much as they can
For this Fendable Foldable
Do-what-you're-toldable
Easily moldable
Buy-what-you're-soldable
Washable Mendable
Highly dependable
Buyable Saleable
Always available
Almost unbreakable
Twistable Turnable Man.

Shel Silverstein

> Which parts of your body can you
> twist and turn?

17

WORK IT OUT

It was a bright and sunny day when Jason cycled out onto the freshly gravelled road after his ball.

The car was travelling at 20 miles per hour and when the driver saw him Jason was 15 metres away. She braked hard. The chart shows why she didn't hit him. As thinking distance (6 metres) plus braking distance (6 metres) is less than 15 metres he was safe this time. The driver was very cross.

But what if the car had been travelling at 30 miles per hour?

What if it had been raining?

If the light is bad, thinking distance may have to be doubled as well.

What if there had been oil on the road?

MPH/KPH	Thinking distance (m)	Braking distance in dry (m)	Braking Distance in wet (m)
20/32	6	6	12
30/48	9	14	28
40/64	12	24	48

You can't do sums like this every time you cross the road. So how do you make sure you cross safely?

Sometimes cars look less important if the light is bad and they haven't got their lights on. Don't be fooled! The driver may not pay much attention to you, either.

LOOK, NO ENGINE!

How can you move without an engine?

The skier races downhill. How will she get back to the top?

What makes an enormous balloon like this go up?

Johnny got a shiny helium balloon at the carnival. He let go of the string. What do you think happened? Do you know why?

The land-sailer seems to fly over the beach. The wind-surfer seems to fly over the water. What makes them go?

DOWN YOU GO

What makes these people move?

What makes them stop?

Why does this parachute fall slowly to Earth? What would happen if the person had no parachute?

We learn as babies that if you drop something it falls to the floor, and once it's been dropped it stays dropped.

Imagine a baby's surprise if the rattle didn't drop. This would only happen in **zero gravity.**

Astronauts have to cope with zero gravity during space flights. Think about the problems it creates when they are eating, drinking, dressing, and moving about. Discuss it with your friends.

On the Moon **gravity** is much less strong than on Earth. The baby would have to wait six times as long for the rattle to hit the floor.

> If gravity makes everything fall, why do some things fall faster than others? Try dropping two equal sized pieces of paper, one flat and one scrunched up.

GLOSSARY

Cog
One of the 'teeth' – the bits that stick out – on the rim of a special wheel called a cogwheel, or sometimes on the edge of a bar.

Gear
A system of moving cogwheels which interlock with each other. When the first wheel moves, its cogs push against the cogs of the second wheel and make that one move too. If the two cogwheels are of different sizes the speed of the second wheel is different from that of the first. You can change the direction of a force by using two cogwheels set at an angle to each other.

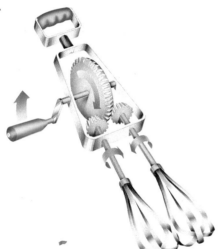

Gravity
Gravity is the force that pulls everything on or near the Earth's surface, or inside the Earth, towards the Earth's centre. Gravity makes things fall when you drop them instead of floating in the air.

Hinge
A hinge joins two parts together in such a way that one can swing towards and away from the other, like a door opening and shutting.

Hovercraft
A craft that travels on a 'cushion' of air. The 'cushion' holds the craft a little above the land or water surface, and is produced by a downwards blast of air. Hovercraft use either a propeller at the back or a small jet engine to make them move.

Pulley
A wheel, usually set in a fixed framework, with a groove on its rim over which a cord can run. Using a pulley is one way of changing the direction of a force.

Scaffolding
A framework of poles and planks used by builders who are putting up or repairing a building.

Zero gravity
Gravity works all the time, everywhere. But when astronauts travel through Space a very long way from the Earth they cannot feel the pull of the Earth's gravity. They can float about inside and outside their spacecraft quite freely, and they feel as if they had no weight at all.